POEMS OF WISDOM

50 Poems Of Wisdom

BY
BEBUH DIVINE

Dedication

I dedicate this book to Christ the living lord the lamb of God who has loved us so much that he gave his life for the salvation of our souls.

POEMS INDEX

ii

01. HARD WORK

He who works hard will not lack.
He will not know shame.
He will not be a beggar.

He who works hard will be distinguished.
He will be outstanding.
He will be the first.
He will leave many behind.

He who works hard will be honoured.
He will stand before kings.
Excellence will become his identity.
He will be a man of dignity.

He who works hard will be successful.
He will be a winner.
He will be sought after.
Nations will knock at his door.

02. LIFE

Life is a test, pass it.
Life is a challenge, face it.
Life is a task, accomplish it.
Life is a gift, take it.

Life is a journey, travel it.
Life is an adventure, engage in it.
Life is a gift, appreciate it.
Life is a puzzle, solve it.

Life is a mystery, believe it.
Life is an opportunity, seize it.
Life is a treasure, value it.
Life is a story, tell it.

03. TIME

Time waits for nobody.
Time respects nobody.
No one can push her around.
She is her own boss.

Time is very hard working.
She never rests.
No pause to eat.
No break to drink coffee.

Time is the best driver.
She does not over speed.
Neither does she slow down.
She is insensitive to the weather.

Time has no regard for kings.
She puts lazy people to shame.
She does not give a second chance.
She is fair to everyone.

Time is just for all.
Time loves everyone.
Time discriminates against no one.
Time loves everyone.

04. TRUE LOVE

True love never dies.
True love never lies.
True love is patient.
True love is kind.
True love hates violence.
True love is gentle.
True love is good.
True love forgives.

True love is not transactional.
True love is not commercial.
True love is special.
True love expects nothing in return.

True love is humble.
True love is pure.
True love is faithful.
True love endures.

True love is caring.
True love is heart-warming.
True love is everlasting.
True love dwells in the heart.
True love is a virtue.
True love is holy.
True love is great.
True love comes from the Christ.

05. LAZINESS

Don't play with laziness she will destroy you
She looks good but is a destroyer of destiny
Laziness is the father of poverty
Embrace laziness and you will soon be a beggar

Laziness makes your life to waste away
A lazy man only watch things happen
He does not know he can make things happen
Stay away from lazy people before they infect you.

A lazy man is like a wind
Every direction is ok with him
He has no value for time
He spends his life entertaining himself.

"Learn from proverbs 20.4 lazy people will end up as beggars Laziness invites poverty proverb 24.33-34"

06. THE HUMAN MIND.

The mind is the greatest resource a nation has.
Many nations foolishly value natural resources over human resources
Invest in your mind and you will be a success

People can steal your money
People can steal you car
People and seize you house
But they can't steal your mind

Invest in your mind you carry it all the time
You can't carry your house on doomsday
Invest in your mind and your living standard will change

The mind is more valuable the gold
More valuable the oil
More valuable than silver
More valuable than timber
Invest in your mind.

07. HONESTY

Honesty brings peace of mind.
Honesty brings peace of heart.
Honesty brings freedom of conscience.
Honesty is so valuable.

Honesty builds life.
Honesty builds nations.
Honesty brings good success.
Honesty saves lives.

Dishonesty is a destroyer.
Bring your life to her, she will ruin it.
Bring your business to her, she will kill it.
Bring your career to her, she will destroy it.

Dishonesty destroys everything in its path.
I have seen presidents fall from the throne because of dishonesty.
I have seen kings dethroned due to dishonesty.
I have seen marriages crash on the rock of dishonesty.

I have seen nations brought to their knees thanks to dishonesty.
Honesty puts dwarfs on the throne, while dishonesty dethrones giants.

Honesty makes the weak strong, while dishonesty brings the strong to
their ruins
Honesty makes the lowly great while dishonesty brings the great to a
shameful end.

08. PRIDE

**Provers 16.18 (Pride goes before destruction,
a haughty spirit before a fall.)**

Pride comes before the fall of any man.
Pride is darkness. Once it comes on you, you can't see.
Pride makes a man forget his humble beginning.
You were once a helpless infant depending on others for survival.
You were once a tiny embryo.

Every man has a humble beginning.
Pride causes man to forget his past.
Pride puffs up a man's heart.
Pride makes a man ripe for destruction.

Herod was eaten alive by worms because of pride.
Nebuchadnezzar ate grass for seven years because of pride.

Pride is a destroyer of destiny.
Have nothing to do with pride.

09. HUMILITY
Mathew 5.5 (Blessed are the humble, for they will inherit the earth. CSB)

Humility is more precious than gold.
Humility precedes true greatness.
Those who humble themselves will be made great.
Those who reject humility reject greatness.

God's promises are reserved for the humble.
Humility is cherished in heaven and on earth.
A humble man serves his neighbour with love.
A humble man never looks down on others.

A humble soul respects the poor.
Those who see themselves as superhumans will be on a dark road.
It is better to be humble than to be proud but if you must be proud,
be proud that you are humble.

10. WONDERFULLY MADE
Psalms 139.14

There is no ordinary human being on earth.
Each one has been fearfully and wonderfully made.
Remember this when evil people tell you, you are ugly.
Remember this when they tell you, you are good at nothing.

If the one who creates you says you are wonderful,
why pay attention to those who did not contribute to your creation?
Don't look down on yourself.
You are beautiful.

You are loved and cherished by God.
You have been wonderfully made.
You have been fearfully made by God.
Jesus loves you as if you were the only one walking on earth.
Jesus loves your neighbour as he loves you.

11. ABORTION
Genesis 25.23

Abortion is the killing of nations according to God.
Abortion is the killing of people.
Abortion is the planning killing and dismemberment of children.

Abortion is evil.
Supporters of abortion are equally guilty.
Innocent children beg to live.
Wicked doctors spill their blood.
Abortion is the worst of evils.
Abortion is the evil of evils.
Denounce abortion.
In the strongest possible terms,
God hates abortion.
He hates the hand that sheds innocent blood.
Authors of abortion are guilty of genocide.

12. TRUST IN CHRIST

Trust in Christ and you shall live.
Rely on Christ as you rely on oxygen.
All who have trusted in him have been exalted.

The more a soul trusts, the more it receives.
Doubt is a rubber of God's grace. Run from her.

God's blessings flow through the door of trust.
If you refuse to trust God you cannot be blessed.
If you trust little, you receive little.
If you trust more, you receive more.

13. FORTY DAYS AND NIGHT

He spent forty days and nights in the desert for my salvation.

The lamb of God endured the hot sun.
He endured cold nights.
He suffered loneliness.
He had me in mind.

I can see my saviour mortifying his body with fasting.
I can see the lamb mortifying his spirit with prayer.
I can see my saviour walking in the desert.
I can see my savour day after day enduring hunger.

He endured the thirst for water due to his thirst to see us saved.
He knew the task ahead was hectic.
The thought of the loss of many souls despite his sacrifice caused him
the greatest pain.
Thank you Jesus, for this sacrifice.

14. THE BLOOD OF JESUS

Oh the Blood of Jesus,
It washes white as snow.
Oh the Blood of Jesus,
It breaks every curse.
Oh the blood of Jesus,
It redeems the soul from its Sins.
Oh the blood of Jesus,
it drives drives demons away.

Oh the blood of Jesus,
It is the cure for man's misfortune.
Oh the blood of Jesus,
It is the gateway to purity.
Oh the blood of Jesus,
It's the drink that brings salvation.

15. FOOLISH INTELLECTUAL

He goes to school and assimilates all he hears.
He never questions or critically analyses knowledge.
He believes his opinion is inferior.
All he hears in a classroom is bible truth.
The foolish intellectual assimilates and reproduces.

He never does an independent study.
The foolish intellectual is a liability to his society.
Only God's word is infallible.
If you are wise you must think critically and validate or disprove
circular knowledge.

16. GOD IS PURITY

God is Purity.
God is the fountain of purity.
God's name is Purity.
God is equal to purity.

God is directly proportional to purity.
God loves purity.
Immorality repels God.
The pure are God's delight.

God's name is Purity.
God elects the pure.
God walks with the purity.
Only the pure in heart enjoy his companionship.

17. A LIVING UNIVERSITY

A living university solves social problems.
A dead university is detached from society.
A living university trains students with skills.
A death university teaches theories which are never tested.
Before you graduate from a living university you are already
working.
Once you graduate from a dead university you become an
unemployed person.

A living university focuses on providing practical solutions.
A dead university specialises in theories.
A living university innovates.
A dead university is stocked with old ideas.

18. KEEP YOUR PURITY

God is purity.
God is the fountain of purity.
Keep your purity, God will honour You.
He who keeps purity keeps God's company.
He who keeps purity keeps his friendship with God.
Blessed are the pure in heart, they shall see God. Matthew 5:8.

Mary kept her purity.God honoured her forever.
Joseph rebuked Potiphar's wife and kept his purity.
God honoured him.
Rebuke your own Potiphar's wife of immorality,
and God will honour you.
Daniel and his friends kept their purity and refused the king's food.
God honoured them.
Consume the gospels and you will be pure.
Jesus says you have been made clean by the words I have spoken to you.

19. GOD LOVES SOCIAL JUSTICE

God is passionate about justice in society.
God yearns to see justice done in society.
He hates injustice.
He wants to see fairness for all.

God yearns for social justice.
He wants to see the widow cared for.
He wants the rights of the blind respected.
He wants to see the lame looked after.

God is passionate about justice in society.
He wants the homeless to be cared for.
He wants the weak strengthened.
He wants to see the labourer paid decent wages.

God is passionate about justice in society.
He wants to see the Hungry fed.
He wants to see the naked clothed.
He wants to see the homeless sheltered.

God is passionate about justice in society.
He wants to see the rights of the orphans respected.
He wants to see the death buried.
He wants to see the oppressed set free.

God is passionate about justice in society.
He wants the rights of the foreigners observed.
He wants to see the elderly people treated with care and dignity.
He wants to see the uninformed instructed in God's way.

God is passionate about justice in society.
He wants to see the sinner admonished.
He wants to see offences forgiven.
He wants to see the doubtful counselled.

God is passionate about justice in society.
He wants to see the sorrowful comforted.
He wants to see the captives set free.
He wants the wicked brought to justice.

20. THE POWER OF UNITY

Woe is he who walks alone.
Two are better than one.
Many hands make work lighter.
Unity makes us stronger.

A united group can easily defeat an aggressor.
A loner is easily defeated.
If you walk in a team you will lift each other up if one falls.
But a person walking alone may never rise when he falls.
The Lord Jesus chose twelve men to walk with him.
Learn from his wisdom and work with a team.
Great things are done by a team, not a loner.

Look for a team and join.
Don't be a loner, if you do then you will soon be a loser.
Unity is strength.

21. POWER OF THOUGHT

As a man thinks in his heart so is he. Proverbs 23.7.
Think big if you want to be big.
Think pure thought if you want to be pure.
Think great in order to become great.

Listen to Philippians 4:8.
God wants us to think of purity.
He wants us to think of love.
He wants us to think heavenly.
He wants us to think of good.

He wants us to think honestly.
As a man thinks in his heart so is he.
We are a product of our thoughts.
Let us think of great good works.
So that we can change the world.

22. SELF ESTEEM

Numbers 13.33 (And we were in our own sight as grasshoppers, and so we were in their sight.)

The world sees you how you see yourself.
If you see yourself as a king, the world will treat you as a king.
If you see yourself as an ant the world will trample on your head.
How do you see yourself?

The men in the desert lost their inheritance to low self-esteem.
Will you also lose your inheritance to low self-esteem?
Rev 5:10, God has made you a king and priest. Will you throw this
blessing away?
Rev 5:10, "And hast made us unto our God kings and priests, and we
shall reign on the earth."

Hold on to God's blessing, hold on to God's promise and refuse to be
belittled.

23. LEADERSHIP

Leadership is about accomplishing a task
not occupying a sit
A leader is limited to his team
Take out time to build good team

Rate a leader by his product
A good leader is seen by product not eloquence
Leadership is not about lavish lifestyle
Leadership is about lifting others up

A good leader must be punctual
She must be God fearing
She must be honest
She must be merciful
She must be accountable

A good leader must be frugal
He must be hardworking
He must strive for excellence
He must be humble
He must be willing to listen and learn.

24. LET CHRIST BE YOUR MODEL

Learn from his heroic humility.
God coming down to wash men's feet.
His hard work, working all day praying all night.

His sacrifice, sacrificing on the cross for us.
His love, giving his entire life for us.
His obedience, doing only the will of the Father.

Let Christ be your model.
Learn from His mercy, raising the widow's only son to life.
Learn from His purity, living a life void of sin.
Learn from His love, giving His life for us all.

Let Christ be your model.
Learn from His forgiveness, He prayed for those who crucified Him.
Learn from His courage, He preached the truth without fear of anyone's status.
Learn from His strong will, He resisted Satan every time his head showed up.
Learn from His honesty, He told us clearly about heaven and hell.

25. Live Each Day As If It Were Your Last

Live each day as if it were your last.

One day you will be right.

Live each day as if it were your last, holding on to Jesus the only true

treasure on earth.

Time is short life is brief.

Live for Christ now, tomorrow may be too late.

Time is running out for all of us.

Spend time with Christ.

Jesus had 33 years and used his time well to finish his work.

Prepare to die.

Life is not certain but death is certain.

Your time is running out.

Reject the falsehoods of earthly riches.

Seek the eternal riches of the gospel of Christ.

26. DEATH IS SURE TO COME

Death is not your end if you have Christ in your soul.
What matters is life after death.
Are you ready to die?
If you are ready to die then you are ready to live.

Continue to trust in the Lord Jesus is the best way.
Care for the needy.
Love your neighbour as Christ has loved us.
Your time is running out.
Love Jesus a lot, get ready to meet the Lord.

27. THE PASSION OF CHRIST

See Christ fasting in the desert, suffering hunger just to save your soul.

See Christ agonising in the garden of Gethsemane just to save your soul.

See Christ sweating blood in the garden just to save your soul.

See Christ suffering severe sorrow of the heart just to save your soul.

See Christ suffering betrayal from His beloved friend just to save your soul.

See Christ arrested with hands tied on His back just to save your soul.

See Christ suffering a night in jail just to save your soul.

See Christ suffering spiritually as He washed the soul of Judas and fell into hell.

See Christ suffering hatred from men, blindfolding, and spat at just to save your soul.

See Christ enduring scourging by evil men, just to save your soul.

See Christ carrying the heavy cross of your sins, just to save your soul.

See Christ falling under the weight of the cross, just to save your soul.

See Christ full of sorrow and He meets his pure, holy and afflicted mother.

See Christ full of exhaustion as He receives help from Simon of Cyrene.

See Christ full of sorrow as He consoles the women.

See Christ suffering our shame as He is stripped of his holy garment.

See Christ suffering excruciating pain as He is crucified on the cross.

See Christ agonising on the cross just to save your soul.

See Christ dying on the cross just to save your soul.

See Christ pierced in the side just to save your soul.

See Christ bleeding blood and water from His heart, just to save your soul.

See Christ on the cross, giving us blood and water as a fountain of mercy.

Wash your soul mind and body daily with this precious blood and water.

Wash your spirit with this blood and water that purifies souls.

See Christ buried in the tomb, just to save your soul.

See Christ risen from death on the third day, just to save your soul.

See Christ ascend into heaven demonstrating victory over sin and death.

See Christ sitting gloriously at the right hand of the Father eternally

Amen.

28. GIVE YOUR ATTENTION TO GOD

A man is what He gives his attention to.
Pay any price to give your attention to God.
We live in a world of distraction.
Pay any price to give your attention to God.

Man's life is like vapour.
It passes away fast.
A day lost cannot be regained.
Give your attention to the one who loves you.

Christ is the only one who truly cares.

29. MERCY

Ask for God's mercy. He will help you.
Be merciful, and you will obtain mercy.
Completely trust in Christ.
Mercy is the greatest work of God.

Be merciful for our Father in Heaven is merciful.
Be merciful to the downtrodden.
Be merciful to the widow.
Be merciful to the orphan.
Be merciful to the blind.
Be merciful to the lame.

30. Our Need For God

Unless God builds the builders build in vain. (Psalm 127.1)
Unless God protects the watchmen are wasting their time.
We need God to eat.
We need God to breathe.

We need God to walk.
We need God to talk.
We need God to dress.
Many believe they need God only in tough times.

No, we need God all the time.
Give God your time.
Give Jesus your time.
Give the holy spirit your time.
God can help you make good use of your time.

31. PRAYER

Prayer is sharing God's goodness.
Prayer is drawing virtue from God.
Prayer is tapping into God's purity.
Prayer is enjoying God's company.

He who prays much will be saved.
He who little is in danger.
He who does not pray will be lost.
He who prays is God's delight.

Two men were crucified with Christ.
One of them prayed and was saved.
The other refused to pray and was lost.
If you pray you will be saved.
If you don't pray you will perish.

32. TAKE CARE OF YOUR ENVIRONMENT

Prayer is sharing God's goodness.
Prayer is drawing virtue from God.
Prayer is tapping into God's purity.
Prayer is enjoying God's company.

He who prays much will be saved.
He who little is in danger.
He who does not pray will be lost.
He who prays is God's delight.

Two men were crucified with Christ.
One of them prayed and was saved.
The other refused to pray and was lost.
If you pray you will be saved.
If you don't pray you will perish.

33. Africa Unite
Ecc 4:9-12

Africa Unite.
Our strength is in our unity.
Africa Unite.
We need one another to grow.
Africa Unite.
We can only defend ourselves, if we unite.

Africa Unite.
Our existence is at stake.
Africa Unite.
Our freedom is at stake.
Africa Unite.
Our dignity is at stake.

Africa Unite.
Our well-being is at stake.
Tiny nations in the world insult you.
Little kings disrespect you all the time.
Africa Unite.

34. LOOK AT CHRIST ON THE CROSS

Christ is burning with love for souls.
He who meditates on the crucified Christ gets newness of life.
He who meditates on Christ must purge his soul of envy and
selfishness.
Meditation on Christ helps the spirit conquer the flesh.

Embrace humility and give up pride.
Carry your cross and that of your brethren.
Do the works of mercy.
Love the Lord.
Console the crucified Christ who thirsts for souls.

35. GIVE THANKS TO CHRIST.

He does not wait for my prayer.
To bless with good things.
So I must not wait for his blessings.
To give him thanks.

Ma ding wa JESUS.
Mbembe kidi Jesu.
Me do yiddi ma Jesu.

Thank you Jesus.
Thank you Jesus.
Thank you Jesus.
Thank you Jesus.

Amen.

36. THE POWER OF PROCLAMATIONS

By your words, you shall be justified and by your words, you shall be condemned (Matthew 12.37).
Your proclamations have power (Mark 11:22-24).
Tell the mountains of your life to be lifted up.
Cast the mountains of your life into the sea.

Have faith in God.
God is working out the answer.
God sends angels to fulfil proclamations of faith.
Your words have powers.
Be careful with your utterances.

37. JESUS WANTS YOUR HEART

Not your money.
Not your gifts.
Not your labour.
Jesus wants your heart.

Not your car.
Not your house.
Not your land.
Jesus wants your Heart.

Not your wealth.
Not your charity.
Not your wisdom.
Jesus wants your heart.

Jesus wants your heart first.
Then the rest can make sense.
Without your heart your work is nonsense.
Without your heart your charity is nonsense.
Give Jesus your heart first, then the rest.

38. WHAT SAVES IS FAITH

Blessed is he who believes in Christ without seeing.
Happy is he who has faith in the Lord.
Because he believes his hardships will be smooth.
His hand will be blessed day and night.

The unbeliever is doomed.
He walks with scales in his eyes.
Even when he sees God's miracles.
He credits science or nature.

Have faith in Christ.
Today is the day of salvation.
Today is the day of mercy.
Tomorrow is too late.

39. Jesus Is Uncreated Beauty

Jesus is uncreated beauty.
Jesus is infinite goodness.
He is countless mercy.
He is pardon unimaginable.

Jesus is love that never ends.
He does not hide from those who choose his company.
He mourns over unworthy ministers and
grieves over unworthy priests.
Unworthy priests are his sorrow of sorrows.

Jesus hates a divided heart.
He is a jealous husband.
He wants a pure heart.
His name is Love.

40. THE POWER OF GOD'S WORD

The word of God is pure.
The word of God has purifying power.
The word of God has sanctifying power.
The word of God brings life.

The word of God is Spirit.
The word of God is everlasting.
The word of God builds.
The word of GOD is food for the soul.

The word of God is a seed of virtue.
The word of God nourishes the soul.
The word of God is full of power.
The word of God has redemption power.

41. THOSE WHO FORGET THE PASSION OF CHRIST

Those who pay no attention to Christ's passion
will always find spiritual emptiness.
Those who meditate on Christ's passion
will obtain many graces daily.

Jesus always repays love with love.
Jesus repays mercy with mercy.
Jesus repays goodness with goodness.
Jesus repays kindness with kindness.

42. ROLL CALL IN HELL

Who are those in hell today?
Those who were ashamed of the gospel yesterday.
Who are those in hell today?
Those who mocked the gospel yesterday.

Who are those in hell today?
Those who practised sexual immorality yesterday.
Who are to in hell today?
The false prophets of yesterday.
Who are those in hell today?
Those who turned the gospel into a money-making enterprise
yesterday
Who are those in hell today?
The hypocrites of yesterday.

Who are those in hell today?
Those who murdered yesterday.
Who are those in hell today?
Those who practised abortion yesterday.

Who are those in hell today?
Those who practised LGBTQ yesterday.
Who are those in hell today?
Those who fabricated their own gospel yesterday.

Who are those in hell today?
Those who polluted the gospel yesterday.
Who are those in hell today?
Those who stole yesterday.

Who are those in hell today?
The unrepentant liars of yesterday.
Who are those in hell today?
Those who practised witchcraft yesterday.

Who are those in hell today?
The swindlers, blasphemers and adulterers of yesterday.
Who are those in hell today?
The fornicators and drunkards of yesterday.

Who are those in hell today?
The homosexuals and lesbians of yesterday.

43. YOU ARE GOING TO DIE

You are going to die one day.
Be sure of this.
Your heart will beat its last time someday.
Where is your soul going?
You shall take your last breath.

You planned your income.
You planned your retirement.
You planned your golden years.
Have you planned your eternity?

You are going to die.
You are a visitor on earth.
This is not your home.
Don't be too attached to this place.
People better than you have died.
People younger than you have died.
People wiser than you have died.
People greater than you have died.

You are going to die.
Put your trust in the everlasting Christ.
He has no beginning, he has no end.
He is the same yesterday today and forever.

Live each day trusting and believing in Christ.
Christ is the only hope for everlasting life.

44. GOD IN YOU

If you abide in Christ He will give you what you ask.
So the task is to abide in God.
The task is to allow God's word to live in you.
Read and meditate on the Bible.

Consume the gospels.
Speak words of faith.
Speak words of hope.
Speak words love.

45. MAKE A GOOD CONFESSION

ROMANS 10:10 "**For it is with your heart that you believe and are justified, and it is with your mouth that you profess your faith and are saved.**"

Make good confessions
Make confession of success
Make confession of healing
Make confession of love

Make confessions of blessing
Make confessions of hope
Make confessions of prosperity
Make good confessions all the time

46. BY HIS WOUNDS WE ARE HEALED
ISALAH 53:5

We are healed by Christ wounds
We are blessed by His suffering
We are comforted by His affliction
We are purified by His precious blood
We are made hold by his chastisement
Praise be to Christ who bore it all
Praise be to christ who suffered for us
Praise be to Christ who paid the heavy debt of our sins

47. LOVE WITHOUT EXPECTATION

Love without expectation earns God's love.
God does not reward transactional love.
Jesus says, do good to those who hate you,
and you will receive blessings from God.

If you love only those who love you,
what have you done out of the ordinary?
Evil men love those who love them.
Even witches share their food and drinks.

Love those who cannot pay you back (Luke 14:12-14).
Interact with people below your class.
Love those who are not in your income bracket.
Learn from Cornelius who loved without expectation and was blessed
(Act 10.1-48).
Learn from Dorcas who loved without expectation and was blessed
with another lifetime (Act 9:36-43).

48. TRUST CHRIST AND LOVE PEOPLE

Reasons why you must trust God not man

God curses any man who trusts in man(Jer 17:5-8).

God has life in himself,

Man does not have life in himself.

Man lives because God lives.

John 14.19 "Because I live you shall live also…"

God is the same yesterday today and forever.

Man is not.

God has no beginning and no end.

Psalms 90.2 "From everlasting to everlasting thou art God."

Man has a beginning and an end.

God has no limits to his authority and power.

Man's power has limits.

God grants an audience around the clock to mankind.

No man can grant an audience around the clock to mankind.

God neither sleeps nor slumbers (Psalms 121:4).

Behold, He that keepeth Israel shall neither slumber nor sleep.

Every man sleeps and slumbers.

49. LOVE ONE ANOTHER

Jesus wants us to love one another as He has loved us.
God is love. God is greater than all.
Love is greater than all.
Let the love of God lead.

God wants self-giving love.
Self-sacrificing love.
Seek to serve others and you will be serving God.
Three things that will last; faith, hope, and love.

50. HOW TO LOVE CHRIST

You love Christ by keeping his commandments.
He who keeps His commandments loves Him. (John 14:15)
His commandments are more valuable than gold and silver.
His commandments are more precious than diamonds.

What are His commandments?
Love your neighbour.
Be merciful to one another.
Uphold purity and humility.
Seek justice at all times.
Care for the oppressed, widows, orphans, and needy.

APPRECIATION

I will to appreciate God who inspired me to write these poems
I want to acknowledge materials that helped me accomplish this work
1. The Holy Bible
2. The teachings of countless men and women of God in books and video tapes
3. The revelations of Christ to katja rivas
4. The teaching of Gods major prophet Tb Joshua.